Individual Travel Protective Measures (ITPM) and Other Helpful Hints

Individual Travel Protective Measures (ITPM) and Other Helpful Hints

for International Work and Excursions

John Weaver

Copyright © 2010 by John Weaver.

Library of Congress Control Number: 2010915671
ISBN: Hardcover   978-1-4535-8608-2
               Softcover   978-1-4535-8607-5
               Ebook   978-1-4535-8609-9

All rights reserved. No part of this book may be reproduced or transmitted in any form or by any means, electronic or mechanical, including photocopying, recording, or by any information storage and retrieval system, without permission in writing from the copyright owner.

Traveling outside of the United States can be inherently dangerous. Use of the tactics, techniques, and procedures covered in this book are no guarantee for success. Techniques are based on generally accepted practices that have been used by various government organizations and militaries throughout the world to help safeguard their members traveling and working abroad. That stated, implementation of these tactics, techniques, and procedures could result in injury or death. Use them at your own risk.

This book was printed in the United States of America.

To order additional copies of this book, contact:
Xlibris Corporation
1-888-795-4274
www.Xlibris.com
Orders@Xlibris.com

Contents

Chapter 1: Introduction 11
    a. Being the "gray" man 11
    b. Becoming a "hard target" 12

Chapter 2: Three Months before Departure 15
    a. Verification of passport (current through your visit) 15
    b. State Department 16
    c. CDC Web site 17
    d. CIA Web site 18
    e. Library 18
    f. Hotel nuances 18
    g. Safety and security 18

Chapter 3: One Week to One Day Prior to Travel 20
    a. Passport covers 20
    b. Travel document pouch 20
    c. Avoidance of wallet and purses 21
    d. Cell phones 21
    e. International adaptor (for charging / using electronic devices) 22
    f. Notify credit card / bank that you will be travelling overseas 22
    g. Local currency 23
    h. Laptops 23
    i. Word-picture portfolio 23
    j. Luggage 24
    k. Motion sensors 24
    l. Charley bar 24
    m. Doorstops 25
    n. First aid kit 25
    o. Survival kit 25
    p. International driver's license 26
    q. N95 face mask 26
    r. Addresses and maps 26
    s. Car rentals (initial) 27

Chapter 4: Modes of Travel 28
    a. Air travel 28
    b. Ground travel 29

Chapter 5: Hotel Considerations 33
    a. Hotel floor 33
    b. Hotel room location 33
    c. Hotel room position 34
    d. Locks 34
    e. Leaving your room 34
    f. Telephone (room) 34
    g. Local hospital and police 35
    h. Rally (meeting) points 35
    i. Hotel windows and sliding glass doors 35
    j. Going to/from room 35
    k. Emergency exits 36
    l. Peepholes 36
    m. Documentation 36
    n. Hotel safe 36
    o. Motion sensors 36
    p. Doorstop use 36

Chapter 6: Out and About 37
    a. Bank Machines 37
    b. Restaurants, markets, stores, and tourist destinations ... 37
    c. Passive surveillance 38
    d. Vehicle parking 40

Chapter 7: Conclusion 41

Appendix A: Checklist/Packing List 43

Appendix B: How to not "look American" 56

Biography 57

Bibliography 59

Dedication

I want to express my love and gratitude to my family. Rarely have I seen a spouse and children that have had to endure months of separation from their husband and father. Therefore, out of my appreciation for all that my family has endured since that dreadful day of September 11, I dedicate this book to my wife, Lisa, my son, John Patrick, and my daughter, Megan. God owns my soul, but Lisa—you own my heart. Thank you all for supporting me over the years and in the endeavor of putting this book together.

Preface

Traveling outside of the United States provides us with wonderful opportunities to experience the world. Through vacationing and working abroad, we have a chance to experience different cultures, partake in cuisine endemic to certain regions and see first-hand landmarks of historical significance. However, it is different from visiting and working in locations within the United States. One must consider the challenges associated with language barriers (provided that you don't speak the language of the location to which you are visiting), lack of conveniences (like twenty-four-hour pharmacies and shopping), currency differences, lack of acceptance of credit cards, and other issues that one must think through. Additionally, traveling to certain locations (even touristy locales) has inherent risks associated with them. The object of this book is to help guide you through the planning and execution of your travels while educating you on how to make you (and your family) a "hard target" to those nefarious characters that prey on the deference and lack of cognizance of typical vacationers and workers. Throughout this book, the terms "trip" and "travel" applies equally to vacationers as it does workers. Though the procedures covered in this book are proven and used by the militaries and other international organizations, it must be stated that these procedures will not eliminate risk all together. Having lived on four continents, worked in nineteen countries, and vacationed in many others, I decided to put together a book that logically walks you through planning for travel abroad.

Chapter 1

The purpose of this book is to cover passive techniques to help safeguard you and your family when travelling outside of the United States. Moreover, it will serve as a guide to help you plan and execute your travel arrangements in order to deflect attention from you (and by extension your family) to someone else. The term "you" will be frequently used throughout this book; the term "you" will be analogous to not just you, but your family as well. Target avoidance is the name of the game. To that end, you will need to carry yourself in a way to make it less palatable to pursue you for the purposes of exploitation. To achieve this, you will have to become the gray man and make yourself a hard target. Careful study of the following must be looked at, practiced, and implemented well prior to commencement of travel. As often is the case with specialized work, muscle memory and learned behavior is what should come across as natural; if you attempt to "execute on the fly," you could find yourself amplifying your American credentials vice mitigating them.

a. Being the "gray" man. The best way to avoid problems is often to carry yourself in such a way as to not be noticed at all. Your demeanor should be both non-threatening and unassuming. Avoidance of staring and unwanted attention should be a desired end state. Essentially, you want to create an image of "belonging" to the local culture (Allied Joint Force Command Headquarters Brunssum, K-1).

   i. The gray man is someone who does not draw unwanted attention to him or herself. In a nutshell, it is blending in and becoming part of the backdrop or landscape of the country.

To become the gray man, you must look at the culture and practices of the general population to the country in which you are visiting. Sensitivity to the culture is paramount. As you conduct your preparation for overseas travel, look to the State Department's country guides and other travel publications on your destination to gather greater perspective into the culture, practices, and dress of that country.

    ii. Prior to travelling, you should look at the clothing (what is and is not acceptable) and practices endemic to the country to which you are visiting (Barth, 155). In the most generalist of terms, this requires one to avoid wearing shorts, white tennis shoes, jumpsuits, socks with Birkenstocks, American sports paraphernalia, religious symbols, and name-brand flashy clothing worn by the quintessential American. Too often, as U.S. citizens, we stand out from other Western contemporaries by the flashy clothing that we wear.

    iii. Identification as an American should be avoided at all costs. Before travelling, it should be incumbent upon yourself to "sanitize" not just your clothing, but documentation and luggage by removing or covering "all things American" (Allied Joint Force Command Headquarters Brunssum, K-1). This will include purchasing baggage without U.S. tags and flags and procuring a generic passport cover to conceal the great seal of our country on this important document.

    iv. Americans are loud by nature. Our Western contemporaries in Europe are much more subdued and soft-spoken than us. Be cognizant of this, especially during check-in at airports, train and bus stations, hotels, and restaurants. After all, it is often during these times, at crowded locations, that those willing to do us harm are most likely watching and studying people as they conduct their "work-ups" for potential targets (Barth, 154).

b. Becoming a hard target (ACM IV Security Services, 6). A certain dichotomy often exists in our world. When travelling, as mentioned previously, you want to be the "gray man." Avoiding the possibility of targeting yourself is the goal. However, at times, others might see through this façade. The other side of the coin involves carrying yourself in such a way that those that might have the inclination to do you harm see that it is best to avoid you and therefore focus on someone else.

i. Presence about you. After you have dressed (conservatively), sanitized your clothing, luggage, etc., of all things American, you should look to carry yourself in a way that shows that you are confident in your demeanor while simultaneously having a keen sense of situational awareness. While becoming omnipresent might not be achievable, to a lesser extent you should be able to show yourself as an individual that knows what is going on around them. To do this involves walking upright, scanning the horizon 180 degrees to the front, and periodically checking behind you. Of equal importance is the avoidance of displaying interesting items to those that would like to prey upon you; items like jewelry, wallets in back pockets and pocket books, electronic gadgets on belts, etc. The desired end state is to have the evildoers of this world focus time and energy elsewhere rather than on you.

ii. Walk on the sidewalk going against traffic (Barth, 157). One of the best practices that you can implement involves walking against traffic. In countries where kidnapping is a prominent business or in areas where insurgents and terrorists want to "roll up" westerners, it is too easy for them to do so while you are walking with traffic. This practice of capturing someone is brought into fruition through an "eye" following you and surreptitiously signaling a vehicle, which will pull up alongside of you. A "snatch and grab" then ensues, pulling you into the vehicle and then taking off. If you walk against traffic, this reduces the vitality of the tactics, techniques, and procedures associated with such practices.

iii. Round corners wide / avoid desolate streets (Barth, 157). When going around corners, take them wide. As mentioned in the last paragraph, an "eye" could signal to someone ahead that you are coming their way. Especially if you round a corner tight to a building, it is less likely that others will see what is going on. If you round a corner wide, you achieve two objectives. First, you can see as you make the turn if something doesn't look or feel right. Second, if someone wanted to grab you, you would force their hand by drawing them into the open, risking their being "made" by other onlookers.

In conclusion to chapter 1, the key take away is that even before you finalize your travel arrangements, you and your family should become familiar with certain things. Being invisible and knowing what is going on around you is critical to maintaining your safety overseas. You want to become the gray man and become a hard target to make it less palatable for someone (or some organization) to do you (and your family) harm. However, it can't be overstated that this requires practice. This is akin to becoming a great baseball player. Practice makes perfect, and you should not wait until game day to put the practice into place. After reading this book, you can also review a fairly comprehensive checklist and packing list in Appendix A at the end of this book (which encapsulates much of what will be covered throughout following chapters).

Chapter 2

Chapter 1 focused on two elementary steps to better prepare you for your travel outside of the United States. We now segue into a more active role in planning your overseas trip. Moreover, we are looking at what should transpire about three months before departure. Understanding that three months is ideal, as a pragmatist, I can appreciate that this luxury might not exist. Nonetheless, the following really should take place prior to commencement of your travel.

   a. Verification of passport. Time and time again, I am surprised to find that those who wish to travel abroad fail to periodically look at the expiration date of their passport. It should be obvious that one must knock the dust off this critical document and review the data to include the expiration date. In a perfect world, the date should take you through an additional seven months (some countries will not admit you if your passport is not valid for at least six months). If not, you should resubmit your application well prior to travel (with requisite photos and other supporting documentation) to have this passport in your possession before travel. During chapter 1, I also covered the importance of ensconcing this document in a generic passport cover to conceal the great seal of the United States. Finally, it is wise to photocopy your passport (and that of your family). Retain these in a locked "TSA approved" suitcase. Though this copy won't get you out of trouble, at least you can present it (and the passport number) to consular services to facilitate the replacement of your passport should the need arise.

b. State Department Web site (www.state.gov). Once you have your passport (you and your family), you can gain a plethora of information from the U.S. government department charged with overseas interface. Some of the areas that should interest you follow.

   i. Country search. Upon gaining access to the State Department's Web site, you should click on the country link. Here you will find great information about the country (or countries) to which you will visit. Specifically, you can ascertain facts on the demographics (religious breakdowns, race and gender statistics, the condition of its infrastructure, and other useful information). This provides a canvass of sorts from which you can glean a better picture of the conditions of which you can expect to see upon your arrival.

   ii. Travel advisories. Actively search for these. If a travel advisory exists for the country to which you will travel, consider cancelling your trip. I cannot underscore the importance of such messages.

   iii. Embassy contact information. Of paramount importance is the contact information of the U.S. embassy that resides in the country of your trip. The telephone number is the most important. Before departing, physically call the number to ensure that it works. Often times, the embassy will list an after-hours number or a connection from the main telephone line; ensure that you know how to contact a living, breathing State Department representative twenty-four hours a day, seven days a week. Generally, when dialing from the U.S., you will dial "011," the country code, city code, and then the number. While overseas, you should also call the number from your hotel so that you understand the idiosyncrasies of telephoning in the new country. For example, if you are visiting the Netherlands, the number listed could be 0031-46-443-0687. When dialing from the U.S., you would dial 011-31-46-443-0687. While in the country, you might drop the first five digits and add a "0" before the sixth digit and dial 046-443-0687.

iv. Registering your trip. The State Department also allows you to register your trip abroad. This is a good opportunity for you for several reasons. First, it provides notification to our government of the time frame in which you will be abroad (and others that will be with you). Secondly, during natural disasters or periods of emergency, it assists the Department of State in, one, finding you and, two, extricating you if conditions warrant an evacuation or rescue of U.S. citizens. Depending on your adeptness with the language (and/or the lack of availability of English-speaking news services), you might not be aware of ensuing conditions until it is too late. You want to ensure that our government can reach out to you for assistance if conditions call for this.

v. Visa requirements. Another overlooked requirement is the need for a visa (whether for work or pleasure). In some instances (like Russia), it could take several months.

c. CDC Web site (www.cdc.gov). Americans are quite fortunate because we live in a society rid of some pesky and debilitating diseases that are endemic to other regions in this world. The Center for Disease Control has an excellent link on its Web site to help promulgate the conditions that one can find in other countries.

i. Vaccination. More specifically, it provides recommendations for inoculation to help prevent the onset of certain diseases, provided that you take the time to become immunized before travel. Likewise, in order for certain medications to be effective, you might be required to receive a shot (or series of shots) well in advance of your travel. Obviously, only a doctor can make the call on this based on your unique medical conditions (and allergies).

ii. Medical Information. Other unique conditions like the state and condition of hospitals and medical facilities can also be found on the CDC Web site.

d. CIA Web site (www.cia.gov)

   i. Country search. Just as was the case with the State Department, the Central Intelligence Agency has information on countries as well.

   ii. Threats. Certain threats and conditions pertaining to travel (not covered by the State Department) can be found by reviewing the facts (from a different perspective), further expanding your knowledge on the picture of the country.

e. Library. You should visit the library or purchase a book on the country and city to which you are visiting. This will give you a better understanding of the culture, practices, and other idiosyncrasies of the people with whom you will visit.

f. Hotel. Proper hotel selection is viewed as a key center of gravity regarding your trip abroad. Painstaking efforts should be made with meticulous searches and reviews to help guarantee your security while mitigating the risks (especially in the higher threat countries). Call the hotel and ask them about their procedures. It is probably prudent prior to making reservations, to also review the hotel section in chapter 5 as it relates to the floor, room location and room orientation.

g. Safety and security. This should be your number one criteria when selecting a hotel. Regardless of the threat (high-profile kidnappers, insurgents, terrorists, and criminals), the security infrastructure is the most important inhibitor to those wanting to harm westerners. Ask the hotel if they use closed circuit cameras (outside, covering the grounds and parking, as well as inside the hotel in common areas and stairwells). As mentioned in chapter 1, though it is not a foregone conclusion, often unscrupulous individuals will pass up hotels with active and passive security measures for those that present a softer target.

   i. Gates. Nothing serves as a deterrent more than a gate. However, the gate must be used to be effective.

ii. Security guards. A more active measure involves the use of security guards. These guards should not just man static positions but should actively search the grounds at irregular timings (those looking to target hotels will most likely avoid hotels employing active patrolling for those not doing so).

iii. Closed parking. This is critical from two perspectives. One, it will help reduce the possibility of tampering and theft of a rental car. Secondly, it will help reduce the likelihood of a vehicle-borne improvised explosive device from being postured for detonation.

iv. Reservations. When making reservations, request a room that is not facing the main road or parking lot (Allied Joint Force Command Brunssum, K-4). Ideally, you should request a room between the second and fifth floors; we will cover more on this in chapter 5. Finally, confirm your reservation; have the hotel e-mail it to you (electronic copy) and print one (hard copy) to retain with your travel documents.

v. Emergency service phone numbers and addresses. Try an Internet search to determine the phone number and address for the local hospital, dental facilities, and police station. Print this out and keep it on you at all times during your travel. Verify this information with the hotel receptionist upon check-in. Upon verification, you might want to add these numbers to your cell phone (for speed dial in an emergency).

vi. Internet. Ask if the hotel offers Internet (and what the requirements are). This can be used as a contingency means to communicate with the outside world in an emergency. Also inquire as to the type of connection offered (secure wireless, DSL, or dial-up).

Chapter 3

Preceding this chapter, we covered the nuances of what one should consider several weeks prior to travel. As you approach travel day, there are certain things that you should look at to ensure that your affairs are in order. The next several paragraphs will help you navigate through last-minute minutia to ensure that you (and your family) are postured for success. More specifically, this looks at the week prior to the day of departure. When considering the first aid kit and survival kit (and components), use these at your own risk (ensuring that you know how to properly use all medication and components before doing so).

> a. Passport covers. We touched on this in chapter 1. If you haven't done so, I recommend that you purchase passport covers to help reduce the telegraphing of your U.S. signature. People are inherently nosy. While standing in line, a passive observer will notice that other onlookers will frequently look at the travel documents (to wit the ubiquitous passport) to determine a person's point of origin. Though by far most of these busybodies are of no threat, there are those that are canvassing crowds looking for targets. To help reduce this threat, a simple passport cover will help cover the U.S. seal, reducing the likelihood of an onlooker making you and your travel companions as American. Thus, you are implementing a great passive technique, helping to keep you "gray."
>
> b. Travel document pouch. Under the category of "hard target," keeping your money, credit cards, and travel documents as safe as possible would be to use a travel pouch (Barth, 156). More to the point, this pouch should be worn around your

Individual Travel Protective Measures (ITPM) and Other Helpful Hints

neck and under a shirt/jacket. Like the passport cover, this is a simple device that is relatively inexpensive. Though this doesn't obviate the need to maintain a keen "presence," it will send a tacit message to criminals to look elsewhere; after all, why risk stealing from someone who has thought of pickpockets when there are so many other unsuspecting people just ready to succumb as prey?

c. Avoidance of wallet use / purse use / sanitizing of "pocket" litter (Allied Joint Force Command Brunssum, K-1). Avoidance of wallets and purses is absolutely critical. Using wallets and purses is tantamount to sending an open invitation to criminals, especially in the busiest of cities and towns. The transference of money, credit cards, ATM cards, and other travel documents to a pouch from a wallet / purse also forces you to eliminate pocket litter. Pocket litter (commonly found in wallets and purses) provides intimate knowledge of you (friends, phone numbers, user IDs, and passwords, etc.), which furthers the likelihood of identity theft and other misfortunes from occurring.

d. Cell and mobile phones—cell phone bands (use of your phone overseas). Today, most of us are inextricably tied to a virtual umbilical cord—the cell phone. Frequently, our lives gravitate around these "mini offices" by another name. However, the U.S. is almost exclusively on a band that is not found anywhere else in the world. Ideally, if you wish to use your cell phone overseas, you must check to see if it is a multiband phone (quad band phones are most likely to be used the world over). You can superimpose this information against a cell band chart to determine compatibility with networks abroad. Furthermore, you should contact your cell provider to see if they can provide coverage while you are abroad. If not, you can look to replace your SIM card upon arrival in a country and use a pay-as-you-go service. Additionally, you must remember to charge your phone. You must determine whether or not your phone can be charged while outside of the United States. Realize that most countries operate on 220 volts (not the 110 found in the U.S.). To charge the phone, you will require a special adaptor (more on this later). Another contingency that you can implement is to ask your provider for a "world phone" and have them provide you one via FedEx or some other overnight provider prior to commencement of travel; remember to "test" your phone before departing. Be forewarned, much of the earth's land mass (actually, most of it) is not covered with cellular towers, hence, regardless if you have the right phone, it would not work. Ensure that you are password protecting your phone when not in use. If you are travelling and/or working in remote locations where mobile service might not be available, you could consider renting a satellite phone. That stated, ensure that you avoid pitfalls with satellite service to ensure that the carrier which you are considering offers service in the region to which you will travel. The Web site wiki.com can provide greater introspective into the cell bands and land-mass coverage of the world.

e. International adaptor (for charging / using electronic devices). U.S.'s two-pronged flat plugs are only found in the U.S. Most countries use a two-pronged round version, though several other variants exist as well. Many travel stores (in airports) will sell international adaptors. The best that I have used exists as a single unit with multiple variants that are attached to that single unit. Query the web to find the prong used in your area, but remember that some countries have two variants. Contact your hotel to verify the outlet used prior to traveling.

f. Notify credit card / bank that you will be travelling overseas; ensure cards don't expire while overseas. In recent years, I have found out too late (after arriving in country) that my credit card is not good because the company has assumed foul play, that someone is exploiting my card. To reduce the likelihood of this, it is imperative that you contact your credit card company(ies) and bank(s) to inform them of your travel (location and dates) to reduce the challenges associated with time zone differences and expensive overseas calls (at exorbitant rates). Another good rule is to ensure that your cards are good for at least six months after your travel dates. Furthermore, contact the hotel to find the providers of ATM services in the country to ensure card compatibility.

g. Ensure that you have several hundred-dollar equivalents of local currency. Nothing is more frustrating than arriving at an overseas locale at a late hour only to find the currency exchange is closed and that your ATM does not work. See your bank and request/have several hundred dollars worth of local currency in your possession to get you through the first few days (incidentals like cab fees, meals, etc.); at the earliest opportunity, test the ATM card (to ensure that it works before you run out of money).

h. Laptops (wireless, high-speed DSL, dial-up cable). If you are planning to take a laptop along for your adventure, it would be best to prepare for some contingencies. This is true in two areas. To begin, if you have a three-prong plug, ensure that your international adaptor will receive this (and more importantly, that your laptop can handle the electrical current of the country). Secondly, it is naive to assume that wireless will be available. I recommend taking both an Ethernet cable and an old dial-up cable as backups, especially if communicating via e-mail is important. If wireless is provided, verify that it is on a secure network (requiring access code or password) to help minimize the likelihood of others viewing your material. Ensure that you are using password protection to safeguard your information when not in use. Furthermore, encryption of sensitive documents and/or files adds an extra layer of security. Password protection and encryption are equally important to memory sticks (flash drives), external hard drives, and other peripheral devices containing sensitive information about you (your family and business).

i. Download word-picture portfolio to assist in communications. If you lack the language skills of the nation to which you are visiting, you might want to download a word-picture portfolio from the Internet. These portfolios are compact and can be pulled out during times where communication with host nation citizens is tenable at best. These word pictures are usually broken into several categories. These include, but are often not limited to, the following: hotels, restaurants, travel (bus, train, cab, and airplane), emergency services (police and fire), banking, recreation, and more. This is just one more tool to help get your through some sticky situations that could arise during your forays abroad.

j. Luggage (hard-shell suitcase with combination lock, rubber seal, and wheels). Though these suitcases are not the most aesthetically pleasing, they can really save the day. A hard-shell case will better protect the contents within it (more so than a canvass or material shell). What's more is that these often come with a rubber seal to help further safeguard the contents, especially during periods of inclement weather. Airport services abroad can be quite interesting. Frequently, I have seen a single-luggage train servicing many planes. If the baggage is removed and placed on the tarmac and it happens to rain, there is nothing you can do. You must acquiesce to the airport personnel to secure your bag. The last thing you want is to have all of your contents (i.e., your clothes) saturated at the outset of your trip. Finally, a locking mechanism can help serve as a deterrent (remember the tenet of becoming the hard target in chapter 1); you can set the lock to a number that you can remember (like your height in centimeters) to see if someone has tampered with the lock (though this is not foolproof since professionals will reset the numbers to what was displayed). Finally, avoid using labels with names and addresses; stick to a contact phone number). Most likely, thieves will bypass your bag for a piece of luggage less intrusive than yours.

k. Battery-operated motion sensors (times two). This helps serve as a deterrent. Motion sensors can be purchased at most electronic stores. Though this won't prevent break-ins, it will definitely startle anyone looking to access your hotel room. These are small and lightweight, and most operate on 9-volt batteries. For a few dollars, you can sleep better, knowing that this additional layer of security stands ready to help you retain the status of becoming a hard target.

l. Charley Bar (Melton, 51). If you find that your hotel room has a sliding glass door, a wood dowel can be used in the track of the door to further augment the locking mechanism of the door itself. My recommendation would be to go to a home improvement store, have them cut a five-foot (by one inch) dowel into the following sections (to build to the door's specifications): 2 ft, 1 ft, 1 ft, 6 in, 3 in, 2 in, and 1 in.

m. Buy rubber doorstop (Melton, 51). The typical hotel room will swing in (inside your room). A great technique to augment the door locks is to simply purchase a rubber door stop and insert this at the door's bottom edge. This provides another layer of protection, helping to facilitate your security, especially in high-risk areas, where you might not be sure who has access to the keys to your room.

n. First aid kits (Allied Join Force Command Brunssum, 3-3). The old adage goes, "an ounce of prevention is worth a pound of cure." As we begin this section, it is a must that you consult a physician for the specific requirements of you and your family. Moreover, careful planning should be done to ensure that you have adequate prescription medication (to last at least one month following your proposed end of trip). You should also consider purchasing a small first aid kit. This kit will not obviate the need for professional medical treatment (in extreme emergencies) but will serve as a bridge (in some cases) to cover you until first responders can address the issue more properly. Generally, a kit should consist of first aid instructions, gauge pads, Band-Aids, butterfly stitches, antiseptic ointment, Motrin, aspirin, medical tape, a needle, and matches. Further consideration should be placed on tweezers, rubber gloves, Imodium (anti diarrhea), Dramamine, antacid tablets, and anti nausea tablets. If the kit is small enough, you can keep it in a pocket (or in a backpack / day pack). As I previously stated, consult a physician before implementing anything in this section. Though I am not a trained medic, my experience has shown me numerous times that having this kit helps significantly during the travel. This is especially true in areas where the adequacy of medical treatment care is suspect at best.

o. Survival kit. This further augments the requirement for a first aid kit. Specifically, a survival kit will have components necessary to help maximize one's likelihood for living another twenty-four hours to three days. As a trained survivalist, it is incumbent upon an individual to practice using these tools to ensure that one knows how to adequately utilize them. Practicing in a local park setting (or even your backyard) will provide better insight into how to do this more effectively vice trying to learn these techniques on the fly. General categories of kits could include the following: tin (to hold components, wrapped and sealed in vinyl tape to make it watertight), survival instructions, water (one-liter water bags, water purification tablets for ten liters; tin can be used to boil water), food (fishing line, hooks and sinkers, and a snare wire/wire saw—verify legality by contacting State Department) for trapping, tools (small pocketknife—verify legality through State Department, P-38 can opener, needle / thread / safety pins, small roll duct tape, and wire saw), signal (signal mirror and whistle), fire (matches and steel/flint also used for cooking, signal, and boiling water), navigation (compass), and, finally, shelter (space blanket wrapped around the survival tin in 550 cord). Survival kits should travel with you (in a backpack or a vehicle glove box).

p. International driver's license (Allied Joint Force Command Brunssum N-1). Having this in your possession will help you ease through the rental car process when travelling outside of the United States. Complementing the traditional license from your state, this document is well received at most overseas locations. I highly recommend obtaining one before the start of your travel (even if you don't have intentions of driving). This is just another tool, providing you with flexibility should the need arise.

q. N95 face mask. This is a recently new addition. These are inexpensive yet critical to filter solid particulates from the air during periods of natural and man-made disasters. Moreover, smog generated from fires to dust and debris following explosions can be inherently dangerous if ingested into your lungs. These masks can help you get through the affected area until you can breathe fresh air once again.

r. Addresses and maps. Prior to travel, you should have the addresses of the hotel, airport, U.S. embassy, work locations, and other relevant locations already printed out and in your travel pouch. Not only can you use these for a GPS, but you can also provide them to locals to assist you in your travels (especially if you can't speak the language). Additionally, you might want to download Internet maps of city centrums and/or acquire travel maps from a local library (or via a bookstore) prior to going overseas.

s. Car rental (initial). If you know that you are going to rent a car, it is best to reserve one prior to departure. Request a nonflashy car in a neutral color (tan, white, gray, or silver); we will cover more on this in chapter 4. Simultaneously, you should request a GPS from this same company (with instructions and maps in English). Print a copy of the receipt and keep it with your travel documents. Pack a tire-pressure gauge to check this upon arrival (all four tires, plus the spare).

Chapter 4

Prior to this chapter, most of what we have discussed centered on the preparation phase of your travels. Most of this work should have been done prior to boarding a mode of travel to your foreign destination. This chapter focuses on general modes of travel and general considerations to help ensure your survivability. We will omit one mode, which bears unique consideration—travel on water (ships, ferries, and boats).

    a. Air travel. In most cases, travel to overseas destinations will involve air travel. Careful consideration should be placed not just on seating but on the requisite documentation (and restricted items) necessary to secure access to the plane. Remember that you can't have liquids exceeding three ounces. Additionally, items found in first aid and survival kits (chapter 3) are prohibited from being taken aboard aircraft.

        i. Seats closest to fuselage. To ensure the maximum chances of survival during a hostage-taking scenario, you want to be seated as close to the fuselage as possible. Terrorists have a tendency to work over those on the periphery of the aircraft. Stated another way, those closest to the aisle are most vulnerable for exploitation. When arriving at the ticket counter, do what you can to avoid aisle seating (ATFP Level 1 Web site)

        ii. Seat by emergency exit (but not actually in the emergency row). Where possible, you will want to be located by emergency seating. This purpose is twofold. One, you have a quicker ability to extricate you and your family from the aircraft after hard landings, crashes, etc. Secondly, seating by emergency aisles will enable you to be moved swiftly off the aircraft as counterterrorist forces work their way through the plane, limiting your exposure to both enemy and friendly fire.

b. Ground travel.

   i. Bus/Train. In the contemporary environment in which we live, improvised explosive devices (IED) are frequently used to attain the ends of nefarious groups of people. Generally speaking, the way IEDs work is that the device is placed at the side of a road and is either self-detonated (that is the vehicle triggers the device by driving over a trigger or passing an infrared beam, likewise triggering the explosion) or command detonated (someone using a hardwired device or wireless devices like a cell phone or radio implements the explosion by pushing a button or series of buttons). The explosion will work its way from the outside in. Therefore, those in the seats closest to the skin of the vehicle are most vulnerable; survival is enhanced by sitting as close to the center aisle as possible. Furthermore, when selecting a train car, you want one that is busy enough to limit your chances of being a victim of crime yet not too crowded (because these train cars have a greater propensity for backpack-style bombs being placed because the collateral damage will bring about a higher payoff than one lesser attended) (ATFP Level 1 Web site). Buses and trains should be avoided at peak travel times (read: rush hour).

   ii. Taxi. Taxis can be a bit challenging even to those with a discerning eye. Cabs can be used by unscrupulous individuals as a cover for exploitation of their personal needs. To minimize this threat, have the hotel (or other business and/or stores) call a cab for you. Upon approaching the car, look to see if it appears to blend in with other cabs of which you have observed. Most cabs will also display the picture identification of the driver; this should match the physical description of the person actually driving the car. If this is not the case, do not enter the car.

iii. Rental car. A sound rental car is of the utmost importance to your security (if you break down in a bad or dangerous area, all the training in the world might not help you arise from and untenable position). If you are looking to rent a car, you should be familiar with the traffic regulations and rules of the host nation. In most other countries, you should be aware of certain nuances. Speeds are covered in kilometers per hour, highway signs are blue rather than green, and there is a proliferation of traffic circles (where those in the traffic circles have the right of way). Do Not Enter signs and other unique markings must be studied prior to getting behind the wheel of a car. Compounding overseas driving involves cars whose steering wheel is on the right side (where drivers drive on the left side of the road); don't forget the stick shift is moved with the left hand (not the right—a whole new dimension). Your vehicle should not be flashy (one that draws attention to yourself); it should also be a neutral color (tan, white, gray, or silver) to make it less susceptible to tailing. When operating a vehicle, ensure that you do so with the windows up and the doors locked at all times. Thieves are quick to grab bags, purses, and other accoutrements while you are stopped; through locking doors and keeping windows up, you reduce the likelihood of being carjacked.

> Inspect outside (tires / fuel cap). This will provide a general indicator to the care of the vehicle. The vehicle should be devoid of major body damage (which could be indicative of more troublesome mechanical issues). Ideally, the vehicle should have a locking gas cap or a door controlled via a lever from within the vehicle (tampering with fuel by adding such ingredients as sugar can cause the engine to seize). Finally, check the tires. Tires should show tread that has not reached the tread indicator bars (if you are unfamiliar with this, visit a tire store and ask the salesman to show you these bars). Furthermore, tires should have no slash marks nor should they show signs of dry rot. Of equal importance is the spare tire (and ancillary items like

Individual Travel Protective Measures (ITPM) and Other Helpful Hints

lug-nut wrenches, jacks, and jack handles); if tires are equipped with locking mechanisms, ensure that you have the key and that this key actually fits your tire. If possible, you might want to procure a can of Fix-A-Flat if sold in the country of your visit or trip.

Engine. Fluids (oil, antifreeze, brake, power steering, windshield wiper and auto-transmission). Fluids are akin to the blood in a body. If these become too low, you risk catastrophic maintenance problems or engine seizure. The aforementioned fluids are the basics that should be checked. Of the fluids, the most important is the oil. It should not show a watery texture nor should particulates (grim/dirt/grit) be present; if this is the case, switch the vehicle out immediately. Additionally, take time to look at the serpentine belt. Cracks should not be present.

Press-on shocks (one bounce). It would be wise to also check the viability of the shock absorbers. By pressing down on each quarter of the car, you can quickly ascertain (in general terms) how good the shocks are. Simply stated, the car should only bounce once. Any more than that and you might have an indicator that the shocks are in a state of poor repair.

Start vehicle (not overheating, starts immediately). The vehicle should crank over with no strain and almost immediately after turning the key, stepping on the accelerator, and depressing the clutch (when applicable) simultaneously. Allow the car to idle for five minutes. The engine temperature rating should fall in the middle (not too high). If the engine overheats while in an idle state, this is not a good sign, and you should request to change your vehicle.

Test drive (take back if not satisfied). Drive around the block. This will provide you an opportunity to see how the vehicle operates (play in the steering, brakes, etc).

Ensure you know how to use the wipers and the lights (to include high beams and hazards).

Heating and air-conditioning. As mentioned in the opening paragraph of this section, it is wise to keep the windows up and doors locked. In chapter 1, we focused on the importance of being a hard target. Since you will be operating your vehicle while "buttoned up," the heating or air-conditioning will be of paramount importance to ensure that the temperature is as comfortable as possible.

Maps and GPS. We covered maps in chapter 3. If you were unable to obtain one prior to departure, most likely you can find one at a local tourist information center. Additionally, you should request a GPS at the time that you order your rental car. Request that the car rental agency provide you with a GPS in English to facilitate your ground movements. However, keep the maps with you as a backup if (or when) the GPS is not working.

Keep your key separate from any information on your name, hotel, and/or license number (to avoid exacerbating problems if you lose your car key).

Chapter 5

In chapter 2, we covered hotels in a generic sense. The express purpose of this chapter is to cover the security setup of your hotel room. This is important for many regards. Primarily, the hotel room will (or at least could) serve as a sanctuary during natural or man-made crisis. What you want to do is "harden" it to the maximum extent, therefore making you (and your room) less vulnerable to criminals, terrorists, insurgents, or kidnappers willing to exploit westerners (for personal or political gain). Upon check-in, ask for the hotel's business card (in English and the native language) and keep this in your travel pouch (it will become very useful in an emergency). Where possible, avoid hotel rooms with balconies and rooms with close proximity to structures and/or trees that can be scaled to access your room.

    a. Hotel floor. As I mentioned in chapter 2, your room should be on the second floor up to and including the fifth floor (Allied Joint Force Command Brunssum, K-4). Avoiding the ground floor is important because many criminals will work a perimeter of a hotel looking for unlocked windows and sliding glass doors. By locating yourself at least one floor above the ground level will serve as a natural deterrent. Generally speaking, fire and rescue equipment is limited to five stories. This is the main reason for not booking a room above the fifth floor. In an emergency, you want first responders to have the ability to rescue you (and your family).

    b. Hotel room location on the floor. The room should be located between the elevator and staircase. The location of your room between these two points provides greater flexibility for getting out of the hotel. Likewise, you don't want to be located too close to the stairwell since many criminals will use the stairwell to attempt to gain access to rooms in close proximity to it (so that if they need to escape, they can quickly exit the hotel).

c. Hotel room position. It should face away from a main road and above the ground parking lot (Allied Joint Force Command Brunssum, K-2). Often times, when vehicle-borne improvised explosive devices are used, they are detonated along the road or in a parking lot. Countless examples show this technique, where a majority of the people that are hurt or killed resided in rooms along the façade, facing the main road and/or parking lot. Residing in a room that is away from the front and above ground parking will help mitigate your exposure to blasts.

d. Hotel locks (electronic key vs. traditional key). Electronic key locks are better than ones using traditional metal keys. However, if your hotel still uses a traditional key, ensure that you keep it in your possession at all times. Metal keys are fairly easy to make impressions (quickly inserting it into a clay mold) for a key maker to use for key duplication, providing someone unrestricted access to your room (Melton, 7).

e. When leaving your room. Request the cleaning personnel to make up your room before departing for the day; only have it cleaned while you are present (Melton, 52). When you leave, make use of the Do Not Disturb sign on the door handle and turn on either the radio or television when you are away. Anyone that is looking to gain unwanted access to hotel rooms will most likely bypass yours.

f. Room phone. Verify that the phone works and you know how to contact the front desk and emergency services. Upon check-in, ask the receptionist how to dial the front desk. In chapter 2, we covered the importance of the phone numbers and addresses for the local hospital and police station. You can verify this with the hotel receptionist (or ask them to provide it for you if you were unable to obtain it before your departure). Understand the dialing instructions; the receptionist can go over the way for you to access an outside line. After you get settled in your room, verify that your phone does work and also verify that you can get an outside line.

g. Hospital, dental treatment facility, pharmacies, and police stations. Know where the nearest hospital, dental treatment facility, pharmacies, and police stations are. Ask the receptionist to mark these points on your map.

h. Rally point (meeting point). Have a rally point for family members to meet during emergency. If you are travelling with your family, you should have a point where you will always meet in an emergency. This is especially true while at the hotel and at other major tourists locations (since tourist locations have a higher propensity for terrorism). Ensure this is outside of the hotel's immediate grounds (at least 250 feet away).

i. Windows and sliding glass doors. Verify that windows lock, use Charley bars to prevent windows and sliding glass doors from opening (Melton, 51). Ideally, your hotel will not have sliding glass doors nor will they have windows that can be opened. However, if you have one or both and they do open; verify that the locking mechanisms are good. We mentioned in chapter 3 that you can make a Charley bar to augment the existing locks of a sliding glass door (by inserting it in the tray of the sliding glass door). If you are not comfortable and/or the locks don't work, request that the hotel move you to another room. Finally, at night, ensure that the blinds/curtains are closed. This will avoid silhouetting yourself for others to see your actions (and identity) by looking up at your room at night.

j. Going to/from room (go up/down flight of stairs and then take elevator). If it appears that someone is observing you in the hotel lobby, you can take the elevator to a floor above yours and walk down a flight to your room (Melton, 51). Likewise, when departing your room, you can walk down one flight and then take the elevator. This will help thwart any surveillance from determining your exact room number.

k. Emergency exits. You might also want to take time to "walk the dog," if you will, by physically walking down the stairs (and out the door if it does not trigger an alarm). This serves three purposes. First, you become familiar with your surroundings. Secondly, you validate that there are no unforeseen blockages or doors that won't open. Finally, you can see firsthand the terrain to which the exit door opens and can better determine a rally point during an emergency.

l. Peepholes. Place a small piece of tape over the peep hole (Melton, 52). This will prevent outsiders from using an amplification device to peer into your room.

m. Documentation. Avoid throwing away sensitive documents. If you have any paperwork with sensitive information (names, account numbers, passport and social security numbers, codes, etc.), ask the hotel if they have a shredder to destroy them for you (Barth, 134). If not, a technique involves ripping the paper into four quadrants. Ensure that a complete number is not found in any one quadrant. Proceed to rip up the contents of each quadrant (retaining the shredded contents in each pile). You can dispose of one quadrant in your room then dispose of the other quadrants (not mixing the contents) in other trash receptacles throughout the hotel.

n. Hotel safe. To maximize the safety and security of your belongings, inquire about the use of the hotel safe (especially if one does not exist in your room).

o. Motion sensors. Orient one toward the window / sliding glass door; the other should face the door. Be careful not to trip these in the middle of the night.

p. Rubber doorstop (Melton, 51). Insert the rubber doorstop to augment your existing locks.

Chapter 6

This chapter covers an eclectic mix of items important for your individual protection yet doesn't fit neatly anywhere else. The bottom line up front is that if you suspect that something is wrong, under no circumstances should you pursue the person that might wish you harm. Contact the local police for assistance.

   a. Bank machines. Most security-conscious people are already aware of a scam that has been running for years. High-tech thieves have created devices capable of replicating and stealing bank cards and their PIN numbers respectively. Most of these devices are a mere façade that attaches to the automated teller machine designed to replicate the card (Allied Joint Force Command Brunssum, K-5). A wireless device then transmits the PIN to a person often waiting in a car. After you have completed your transaction and moved on, the thief recovers the façade, creates a card, and then proceeds to move money out of your account. Be aware as you use ATM machines. Ideally, use them only in secured locations (like inside a bank). Also, look for a device that appears out of the ordinary that is attached to the part of the ATM where you insert your card. Other telltale signs could be an individual (or individuals) in a car within close proximity to the ATM (most likely picking up the signal that would transmit your PIN). If something doesn't feel right, avoid the ATM and move to another one.

   b. Restaurants, markets (bazaars), stores, and other tourist locations. While you are exploring the foreign landscape, remember that often times tourist destinations are targets for terrorists and insurgents. Incidents involving pickpocketing and purse snatches could even be more likely. As stated previously, keep your money/cards/documents on you in a pouch worn around the neck and tucked into a shirt. You might also want to have small exchanges of money in your front pocket (for buying incidentals); often times, those scoping out would-be victims watch people to see from where they are pulling their money. Scams often involve two or more parties where one distracts you. For example, a lady selling flowers—when you lean forward to inspect and smell them, another individual will lift your wallet. Ideally, you want to avoid tourist areas all together. However, if you are still inclined to visit these areas, know where the escape points are, have the local police number programmed in your cell phone (if you have one), and keep your pouch tucked securely against your body. To better prepare for other emergencies, it would be prudent to designate rally points at these destinations as well (when travelling with more than one person). Finally, know where the exit points are; ensure that everyone in your party knows these as well. Designate a rally point (meeting point) at least 250 feet outside of the restaurant, market (bazaar), store, and/or tourist location.

c. Passive surveillance (ACM IV Security, 47). The key behind passive surveillance is to not elicit a response from the person (or persons) tailing you. Whether on foot or in a car, telltale signs arise when a person (or vehicle) seemingly appears and reappears. There are four phases that persons conducting surveillance go through. Phase one—the stakeout phase (usually done around your hotel or workplace). Phase two—the pickup phase (phase where they will start to follow you.) Phase three—the follow phase (when you will notice that you are actually being tailed). Phase four—the box phase (when the persons conducting surveillance will attempt to position people/vehicles around all likely avenues of departure after you have stopped moving, to pick you back up after you start to move again). The following is a breakdown:

   i. Foot techniques (ACM IV Security, 61). The goal is to identify the same person at two different locations for no apparent reason. When turning around corners, take them wide to prevent someone from grabbing you as you make the turn.

Departure. As you depart your residence/hotel/workplace, look casually for personnel at outside stands (newspaper / vendors / bus stops / pay phones), window shoppers, people in the lobby, or others that start to observe your actions as you move. Also, look for vehicles positioned for the pickup phase. Almost always, these vehicles will be parked on the right side of the road, a parking lot on the right side of the road, or a side street on the right side of the road—all to quickly move into traffic to follow you in your vehicle upon your departure. During the stakeout phase is the most likely time when you can passively detect surveillance.

Generally, walk against traffic on the sidewalk (Barth, 157). Staying relatively close to the buildings, arch outward as you are about to cross the street. While performing this arch, discreetly look for people that are following you or who are walking parallel to you on the opposite side of the street. Those following you will usually slow their pace to avoid catching up with you or crossing you. Generally, even those that use disguises will not wear jewels or flashy clothing and will wear the same watch and shoes.

Look for people that seem to talk into their chest (communicating). They will signal other persons by looking at their watch, pulling out a handkerchief, or scratching their head.

ii. Vehicle techniques (ACM IV Security, 51). As you pull out, look for vehicles that pull out behind you along the road on which you are travelling, out of a parking lot on the right side of the road, or a side street on the right side of the road. Surveillance vehicles will generally be nondescript; nonflashy; tan, white, silver, or gray in color.

Some telltale signs involve vehicles that are running (exhaust coming from the tailpipe), two occupants in the front seats (generally males), seatbelts on, and possibly coffee cups / clutter on their dashboard. A trigger vehicle is the first one that will fall in behind you.

The goal is to identify the same vehicle at two different locations for no apparent reason.

Look for mirroring/convoying. This is when a vehicle following behind you moves as you move from lane to lane.

Early move into turn lane. Signal early and move into the turn lane; look for vehicles doing the same.

d. Vehicle parking. When parking vehicles, always park in a lit area (and when possible, keep the vehicle in a secure lot). When possible, back your vehicle into a parking spot (to ease your getaway and to provide you maximum flexibility for getting out of a tight situation). If you park along a curb, turn your wheels into the curb to mitigate the likelihood of a successful tow. Furthermore, keep no valuables (and nothing of consequential value in plain sight) in the vehicle, and lock the vehicle (with the windows up) when you are away. Upon return to the vehicle, conduct a visual walk-around inspection of your vehicle to look for tampering (if you suspect tampering, as you approach the driver's side door, pretend to tie your shoes; while doing so, look under the vehicle and into the driver side's front wheel well for improvised explosive devices). If you suspect tampering, contact the hotel staff or police immediately. Upon entering the vehicle (and after checking the backseat), start the vehicle, lock the doors and move out. Don't sit idly in your vehicle.

Chapter 7

Hopefully you have a better perspective on travel and security considerations associated with overseas forays. What should be clear is that there is a lot of homework and preparation work required to adequately prepare for your trip. What should also percolate to the top of your mind is the vigilance required to operate safely day in and day out while abroad. As mentioned earlier in the book, visiting and working outside of the United States can be inherently dangerous. Consequently, the practice of being the gray man and a hard target can help mitigate the likelihood of bad things happening to you (and your family). Conversely, the practice of what was covered in this book is no guarantee for success; at times, bad things happen to good people. Having a plan and through sequentially working through the travel (three months out, one week out, and then daily while abroad), you stand a better chance at having a successful overseas trip.

Appendix A

Checklist/Packing List

a. Sixty days to one week before travel.

___Visit State Department Web site

   ___Conduct country search

   ___Verify visa requirements

   ___Check for travel advisories

   ___Register your trip on the State Department's Web site

___Visit Central Intelligence Agency (CIA) Web site (country search)

   ___Check threats

   ___Verify information from State Department Web site

___Visit Center for Disease Control (CDC) Web site

   ___Check for inoculation and immunization requirements

   ___Check for conditions of medical care

   ___Consider medical insurance

___Conduct hotel searches (looking at security)

___Make hotel reservation

___Verify expiration date of passport(s)

___Request visa well in advance of travel (if required)

___Notify bank and credit card companies of your trip abroad

___Request currency of the nation to which you will visit (via your bank)

b. One week to the day of travel.

___Locking hard-shell suitcase (with rubber seal and wheels)

___Maps

___Charley bar

___First aid kit (consult a physician before purchasing and using)

___Case

___First aid instructions

___Antiseptic ointment

___Gauge pads

___Medical tape

___Butterfly stitches

___Band-Aids

___Needle

Individual Travel Protective Measures (ITPM) and Other Helpful Hints

___Matches

___Tweezers

___Aspirin

___Motrin

___Imodium

___Anti diarrhea

___Rubber gloves

___Antacid tablets

___Dramamine

___Survival kit (ensure you are properly trained before using)

  ___Survival instructions

  ___Metal case (can be used for boiling water / cooking)

  ___Vinyl tape (to secure lid to case, keeping it waterproof)

  ___Navigation (button compass)

  ___Fire

    ___Matches (waterproof)

    ___Flint and steel

  ___Water

    ___1-liter water bag

    ___Water purification tablets

___Tools

    ___Pocketknife

    ___Wire saw

    ___P-38 can opener

    ___Needle / thread / safety pins

    ___small roll of duct tape

___Food Gathering

    ___Fishing line, hooks and sinkers

    ___Wire saw (for trapping game)

___Shelter

    ___Space blanket (affixed in bag outside of survival kit)

    ___10 feet of parachute cord (wrapped around blanket and kit)

    ___Four zip ties (inside case)

    ___Small roll of duct tape (1 in. x 5 ft.)

___Signal

    ___Whistle

    ___Signal mirror

___Prescription medication

___Over-the-counter drugs (note: these are often hard to come by overseas)

INDIVIDUAL TRAVEL PROTECTIVE MEASURES (ITPM) AND OTHER HELPFUL HINTS

___International electric adaptor

___Umbrella

___N95 protective mask

___Tire-pressure gauge

___20-gallon plastic trash bag (for dirty laundry or emergency waterproof cover)

___Ziploc bags (great for waterproofing electrical devices)

___Travel pouch

___Passport (with travel visa if required)

___Picture identification

___International driver's license

___Proof of car insurance

___Credit card

___ATM card

___Airplane tickets

___Hotel confirmation (with address and phone number)

___Rental car / GPS confirmation (GPS in English)

___Three days of prescription medication

___Local and U.S. currency

___Phone numbers and addresses to local hospital and police

____Phone number and e-mail of your attending physician in the United States

____Dramamine (taken from first aid kit)

c. Hygiene Kit

____Sunblock

____ChaptStick

____Shampoo

____Conditioner

____Razors (1 per week)

____Shaving cream

____Toothbrush

____Toothpaste

____Lotion

____Dental floss

____Deodorant

____Eye drops

____Nail clippers

____Tweezers

____Soap

____Comb/brush

INDIVIDUAL TRAVEL PROTECTIVE MEASURES (ITPM) AND OTHER HELPFUL HINTS

___Hair dryer (correct volts)

___Curling iron

___Cosmetic kit

d. Generic packing list

___Battery-operated (or wind-up) travel clock (with extra battery if applicable)

___Watch with alarm

___Sunglasses

___Wet-weather Windbreaker

___Washcloth (many foreign hotels don't have washcloths)

___Backpack (but only for nonsensitive items like first aid kit, wet-weather jacket, and umbrella)

e. Clothing checklist

___Men

___Underpants

___Undershirts

___Suit coats

___Suit pants

___Belt

___Dress shirts

___Dress socks

___Polo shirts

___Khakis

___Dress shorts (if accepted)

___Jeans

___Dress shoes

___Casual shoes

___Ties

___Overcoat

___Windbreaker

___Work-out shorts / shirts / jacket / sweats / socks / running shoes

___Bathing suit

___Shower shoes (pool)

___Women

___Bras

___Panties

___Stockings

___Dress socks

___Dress shoes

___Dress pants

Individual Travel Protective Measures (ITPM) and Other Helpful Hints

___Belt

___Casual shoes

___Tennis shoes

___Work-out shorts / shirts / jacket / sweats / socks / running shoes

___Bathing suit

___Skirts

___Blouses

___Jackets

___Overcoat

___Windbreaker

___Purse (discouraged)

___Jeans (pants)

___Shower shoes (pool)

f. Rental car checklist

___Reservation printed (nondescript; nonflashy; tan, white, gray, or silver)

___GPS requested (with instructions in English)

___Fluid levels

   ___Oil

   ___Transmission (if automatic)

____Engine coolant

____Windshield wiper

____Brake

____Exterior

    ____No visible damage to exterior (to include windshield and windows)

    ____Check shocks

    ____Locking mechanism for gas tank

    ____Know how to open the hood

    ____Know how to open the trunk

____Tires

    ____All lug nuts present

    ____Tires not worn (check tread bars)

    ____No visible gashes and cuts on outside of wheels

    ____Spare tire (easy access with no locking mechanisms or ensure you have key)

    ____Tire pressure (to standard located on wheel, include the spare)

    ____Jack, lug-nut wrench, and jack handle (all present and working)

    ____Tire key (if tires are equipped with wheel locks)

Individual Travel Protective Measures (ITPM) and Other Helpful Hints

___Interior

    ___Lights work (normal, high beam, reverse, turn signals, and hazards)

    ___Horn works

    ___Seatbelts are operational

    ___Wipers functioning and wiper fluid works

    ___Car starts on first try

    ___Door locks function (keep doors locked when driving)

    ___Windows work (keep windows up when driving)

    ___Adjustable mirrors work

    ___Car rental agreement present

    ___Both air-conditioning and heating work

___Test drive car

    ___Ensure brakes work

    ___Engine does not overheat

    ___Verify fuel type (and side where the gas tank is on)

    ___Ensure all dashboard gauges work

    ___Muffler works, no blue or black smoke emissions

g. Hotel room checklist

    ___Located between second and fifth floor

____Located between the elevator and emergency staircase

____Ensure windows and/or sliding glass door locks work

____Verification that hotel room telephone works (and you know how to dial out)

____Use of Charley bar for sliding glass door

____Activation of motion sensor (for door)

____Doorstopper (augment security of door)

____Use of Do Not Disturb sign and turn on radio/television when departing room

____Verify the emergency exit door works (provided it does not activate alarm)

____Walk staircase to ground floor (no blockage or surprise in event of an emergency)

____Verify that the door to the ground floor (emergency) opens (if no alarm is present)

____Designate a rally or meeting point outside hotel in the event of an emergency

h. Electronic (all items verified by volts and phase for country to which you will travel)

____Laptop with charger

____DSL cable

____Dial-up cable

____Cell phone with charger (if verified for band—keep in your front pocket for walks)

___Satellite phone, charger, extra battery, and vehicle antenna (service activated for country to which you will visit)

___Digital camera (with memory card and batteries)

___Hair dryer / electric razor / curling iron (verified for foreign electrical current)

___MP3 player (or equivalent) with spare batteries (or charger)

___Motion sensor with battery (and spare battery)

___Webcam

Appendix B

How to not "look American"

a. Dress: Avoid logo outfits, tracksuits, white tennis shoes, and fanny packs.

b. Eating: Use fork and knife (at the same time, try to avoid using a fork and knife to cut food and then lay the knife down and switch hands to use the fork); also remember that patience is a virtue (overseas eating takes much longer and customer service is often lacking).

c. Doors: Most doors to buildings overseas open outward.

d. Talking: Tone it down! Talk softly when conversing with others.

e. Avoid wearing religious symbols.

Biography

John Weaver has served as an officer in the United States Army (culminating at the rank of lieutenant colonel) and has over twenty-plus years of experience. Since entering active duty, he has lived and worked on four continents and in nineteen countries, spending nearly eight years overseas (on behalf of the U.S. government). His experience includes multiple combat deployments, peace enforcement, peacekeeping, humanitarian relief, and disaster assistance support in conventional and unconventional / nontraditional units. He has received formal training/certification in the following areas from the U.S. Department of Defense: survival/evasion/resistance/escape (high risk), communications equipment and communications planning (FM radio, landline and satellite communications, encryption, and the use of cryptographic devices), digital camera use and digital photography courses, U.S. Special Operations Command counterintelligence awareness course (USSOCOM CI), joint antiterrorism course, defense against suicide bombing course, homeland security and defense course, the joint special operations task force course (JSOTF), defensive driving course, vehicle emergency drills (battle drills), composite risk management, and more. Additionally, he graduated from NATO's Combined Joint Operations Center course in Oberammergau, Germany. John earned a Bachelor of Arts degree in Business Management from Towson University in 1990 and graduated from Central Michigan University with a Master of Science in Administration degree in 1995.

Bibliography

ACM IV Security Services, *Surveillance Countermeasures, A Series Guide to Detecting, Evading and Eluding Threats to Personal Privacy* (Colorado: Paladin Press, 2005).

Allied Joint Force Command Headquarters Brunssum, *Headquarters Support Group Standing Operating Procedure for Deployed Operations* (The Netherlands : JFC HQ Brunssum Printing and Graphics, 2007).

Barry Davies, *The Spycraft Manual The Insider's Guide to Espionage Techniques* (Minnesota: Zenith Press, 2005).

H. Keith Melton and Craig Piligan, *The Spy's Guide: Office Espionage*, (Philadelphia: Quirk Books, 2003)

Jack Barth, *International Spy Museum Handbook of Practical Spying, National Geographic,* Washinton, D.C.

U.S. Department of Defense, *U.S. Army Survival Evasion and Recovery* (New York: Skyhorse Publishing, 2008).

Anti Terrorism Force Protection Level 1 Web site, *https://atlevel1.dtic.mil/at/*—accessed on September 03, 2010.

Index

A

adaptor, international, 21-22
airport
  address, 27
  personnel, 24
  services, 24
air travel, 24
  emergency exit, 28
  seating, 28
  See also ground travel
American, 12, 17
  how not to be identified as, 11-13, 20, 56
automated teller machine (ATM), 37
  cards, 21, 23

B

bank, 37
  machines. *See* automated teller machine (ATM)
  notification, 22
  See also credit card
bazaars. *See* markets

C

car rental. *See* rental car
cell phones, 19, 29, 38
  network provider, 21
Centers for Disease Control (CDC), 17
  Web site, 17
Central Intelligence Agency (CIA), 43
  Web site, 18
Charley Bar, 24, 35
checklist, 14, 43, 49, 51
  clothing, 49
  departure preparations, 43-44
  electronic gadgets and paraphernalia, 54
  generic packing, 49
  hotel room, 53
  hygiene kit, 48
  rental car, 51
clothing, 12, 39
  checklist, 49
convoying, 40
country, search for, 16, 18, 43
credit card, 9, 20-22, 44. *See also* bank
criminals, 18
currency, local, 9, 23, 44

D

departure, 38-39
departure preparations
  checklist, 43-44
  prior to boarding, 28
  three months before, 15
  week before, 20
disasters, 17, 26
diseases, 17
documentation, 36
doorstop, rubber, 25, 36
driver's license, international, 26

E

embassy. *See* U.S. embassy
emergency, 17, 33, 35-36, 38, 54
  exits, 28, 36, 54
  facilities, 35
  phone numbers and addresses, 19
  services, 23, 34
engine, 30-31, 53

F

FedEx, 22
first aid kit, 20, 49
  contents, 25
  instructions, 25
foot techniques, 38

G

Global Positioning System (GPS), 27, 32, 47
gray man
  to become the, 11, 14
  helping to keep you a, 20
  practice of being the, 41
ground travel, 32
  bus/train, 29
  rental car, 19, 26, 30, 32, 51
  taxi, 29
  See also air travel

H

hard target, 9, 32, 41
  becoming a, 12, 14, 24
  make yourself a, 11
  under the category of, 20
hotel, 12, 22, 32, 35-36, 38-39, 54
  gates, 18
  Internet, 19, 23, 27
  safety and security, 18
  security guards, 19
  selection, 18
hotel room
  Charley Bar, 24, 35
  checklist, 53
  floor, 33
  location, 33
  locks (electronic vs. traditional), 34
  motion sensors, 24, 36
  peepholes, 36
  phone, 34
  position, 34
  rubber doorstop, 25, 36
  safe, 36
hygiene kit checklist, 48

I

improvised explosive devices (IED), 19, 29, 34, 40
insurgents, 13, 18, 33, 38
invisibility, 14

K

kidnappers, 18, 33
kidnapping, 13

L

language barriers, 9
laptops, 23
library, 18
luggage, 12, 15, 44
   locking mechanism, 24

M

markets, 37-38
Medical Information, 17
meeting point. *See* rally point
mobile phones. *See* cell phones
Motion sensors, 24, 36, 55
multiband phones, 21

N

N95 face mask, 26
Netherlands, 16

P

packing, generic list, 49
packing list. *See* checklist
parking, closed, 19
passport, 36
   cover, 12, 20
   verification of, 15
pickpocketing, 38
pocket litter, 21
police, 19, 23, 34-35, 37-38, 40, 47
portfolio, word-picture, 23

pouch, travel, 20
protection, individual, 37
purses, avoidance of. *See* wallets, avoidance of

Q

quadband phones. *See* multiband phones

R

rally point, 35-36, 38, 54
rental car, 19, 26-27
   checklist, 51
   heating and air-conditioning, 32
   inspection of, 30
   key, 32
   maps and GPS, 32
   start-up, 31
   traffic regulations, 30
reservations, 18-19, 51
restaurants, 12, 23, 37-38

S

safety and security, 14, 18, 26, 33, 36, 46
satellite phones. *See* cell phones
scams, 37-38
security guards, 19
shock absorbers, 31
sidewalks, walking on, 13, 39
SIM card, 21
State Department, 12, 16-18, 26, 43
   representative, 16
   Web site, 16, 43
stores, 22, 24, 29, 37
suitcase. *See* luggage

surveillance, 35, 38-39
  passive, 38
survival kit, 20, 28
  general categories of, 26

T

target avoidance, 11
terrorists, 18
tourist destinations, 35, 37
traffic regulations, 30
travel
  addresses and maps, 26
  advisory, 16
  arrangements, 11, 14
  pouch, 20-21, 27, 33, 38
  registration, 17
  threats to, 18

U

United States, 4, 48
  traveling outside of, 4, 9, 11, 15, 21, 26, 41

U.S. citizens. *See* American
U.S. embassy, 26
  contact information, 16

V

Vaccination, 17
vehicle
  parking, 40
  techniques, 39
vigilance, 41
visa, 17, 47

W

wallets, avoidance of, 21

Made in United States
Cleveland, OH
13 January 2025